THE BOY AND THE MONARCH

Sonnets and Variations

by

Emery George

Ardis * Ann Arbor

Emery George
The Boy and the Monarch: Sonnets and Variations
© 1987 by Emery E. George. All rights reserved.
Published in July 1987 by
Ardis, 2901 Heatherway,
Ann Arbor, Michigan 48104
Manufactured in the United States of America.

Library of Congress Cataloging-in-Publication Data

George, Emery Edward, 1933–
   The boy and the monarch.

   1. Sonnets, American.   I. Title.
PS3557.E48B6   1987   811'.54   87-1485
ISBN 0-87501-027-X

Acknowledgments:

Some of the poems in this book appeared previously in magazines and other sources as named below. Grateful acknowledgment is made to all editors, for their kind permission to reprint the poems here.

The Cat and the Moon: "A Little Learning"; *Green River Review:* "Looking for Ezra Pound in Venice"; *Hampden-Sydney Poetry Review:* "A House All Pictures"; *Michigan Quarterly Review:* "Rest on the Flight to Egypt"; *Modern Poetry Studies:* "Homage to Edward Hopper"; *The New Laurel Review:* "Your Friend and Mine"; *Phantasm:* "Standalone"; *Poetry:* "Moiré"; Copyright © 1976 by The Modern Poetry Association. *Raccoon:* "May Walk"; *Song:* "Alexandrite, or Jeweler in Purgatory," "Lights on Earth"; *Spoon River Quarterly:* "Rebirth."

"Projects" and "Grief" appeared in: *The Ardis Anthology of New American Poetry,* edited by David Rigsbee and Ellendea Proffer. Copyright © 1977 by Ardis. "Homage to Edward Hopper" is reprinted in: *The Hopwood Anthology: Five Decades of American Poetry,* edited by Harry Thomas and Steven Lavine. Copyright © by The University of Michigan 1981. Reprinted by kind permission of the publishers, The University of Michigan Press. "A House All Pictures" is reprinted in: *Anthology of Magazine Verse and Yearbook of American Poetry,* 1981 edition, edited by Alan F. Pater. Copyright © 1981 by Monitor Book Company, Inc. Reprinted by kind permission of the editor.

"Homage to Edward Hopper" and "On Silence" appeared previously in book form in: *A Gift of Nerve: Poems 1966-1977,* by Emery George (Ann Arbor: Kylix Press, 1978). Copyright © 1978 by Emery E. George.

This book is inscribed to the memory of

NORMA FARBER
(1909-1984)

mentor and treasured friend,
distinguished author and poet,
nature's knowing listener

CONTENTS

4. Doublesonnets

5. King versus Knave 87

1.

The Boy and the Monarch

The Boy and the Monarch

Mister: are you trying to drive or kill?
That's my light, friend; don't block my path. The morning
sun's in my eye. A butterfly is riding
spread-eagle—Monarch—mounted on his grill.
Caught, with its orange-and-black stained-glass wings,
it looks like a Lucifer crucified.
I see it but a split second. It's dead.
A driver sports his racing trophy. They wrong
each other: an inching victor's victim shown
whole. Winged stars haven't spied on this run of men
since Grandfather Meteor dinned. The meadow's run-on
music is muffled. He hasn't caught a moan—
total silence. Dangerous daydreams:
Monarchs are status symbols of our times.

Americans have always craved a king.
Can it. Your fellow subject will hardly sweat
at pinning you, butterfly-neat, in a suit
for criminal negligence. Drunk driving,
no alcohol. Were tendon, muscle, bone
ready to stop? Did you brake and brace?
Scenarios are bad. And it's no excuse,
saying you drove against the light, alone,
when in your brain cells it was convivial dream.
A Monarch fluttered over meadow grass,
a half-remembered sequence. Film frames pass:
a child runs over a field; you are deaf and dumb;
day, half-blocked, as by Venetian blinds,
looms up ... an inch too late. My gear shift grinds,

the car shrieks to a halt. *(Black-and-orange,*
school colors, complemented by a blue-white sky;
Ming porcelain, over a good log fire,
andirons, coals—unseasonal, and strange ...)
Nonsense. Watch this instead. Now a boy jumps
out from behind a ball, a post—between
our two cars. Again I miss the green
light in order to give the kid a chance.
He pries the butterfly free of that grill
(at least, I think he does. He is earnestly hunched;
I cannot see his hands. I'll bet he gets crunched—
nothing doing. Kids don't know danger). *With skill:*
scratch, pull, gently lift—his, with craving care!
Hands cupped, a child walks off. ... A moving car ...

Boy Struck by Lurching Car. I tell the sergeant
I couldn't see who ran him, who would dare.
It was a warm summer morning. We both just sat there,
behind our steering wheels, missing him by the margin
of a leaf, in our minds. An insect—splat!—
and you live forever. *It happened long ago,*
Officer. I still feel subzero wind blow
up my sinuses. Some devilish plot
forced me, one night, to walk home from the store,
six miles, along a busy highway. I was eight.
I faced traffic, mincing, jumped out of the way,
shaking my fist at each unfolding car:
Go on right through me! I won't feel a thing!
There, runaway imagination was king.

Hospital room. Pray that the boy pulls through.
A bruised spine is no injury at all
nowadays. Brain damage? Can't tell yet. His fall
was all you saw, okay? No sound. One move
can get you hooked on hit-and-run a-mix,
Mister. At Homicide, they don't kid around.
Were there eyewitnesses? Faulty brakes ground
offenders in the clink for months. So relax.
Stonewall. That's better than serving time.
You looked sick as a moth. Your face was white
as our basement floor flooded by moonlight,
my wife tells me. *No cleared husband of mine*
will crash alive, head-on, into the law!
We're fragile butterflies, sir. There's the claw—

all that's past now. The kid is fine. I dream
winter dreams and, this time, stay awake.
Trees glide past; cold fingers grip the wheel. Now watch
the signs. Silos, boarded-up houses, an old drum
(it once held gasoline). Huge water tower ... .
Keep mind and body on the road. A truck throws slop
on fender, window. At curves, with ice, you'll slip
on these country paths. No signs or rail guards here.
You veer an inch, go right over that edge.
Now recollection brings that butterfly
before my blinking eye. Its symmetry
is beautiful, in death or life. A nudge
of memory: it's dance, a man in flight
where earth's and angels' madnesses press you flat,

for here, within me, sits that runaway boy,
in my wild chest, still strapped to seat and wheel
(sir, the better to grill you!); we ride a horse of steel
and glass, self-harnessed, out to help destroy
our fear of flight, of heights, to kill fear of pain.
We travel in manmade cocoons and live
the philosophy of the wheel, in love
with suicide; pinioned of wing, supine,
we long for death—another world and form.
My boy now wants to run and dance and fly.
But what if he were not really a boy
at all? a figure, rather, from a poem,
a paraphrase of a famous line from Yeats?
How can we tell the Monarch from his mates?

*

Beauty and immortality, the twin
angels of death, of life, ensnare a soul
sensitive to names, one to behold
fragile elegance: a pair of wings,
black, ranging to heaven's blue; a Redouté
painting showing white roses, butterflies
in subtle tints of azure, rust, and gray;
clear photographs, engravings. A boy descries
what he cannot describe: color, a shape,
a skilful pattern, nature's clarity;
originals: fresh flowers, a girl. The ache
of admiration is his, uncertainty
as to who is the beauty, who the sage.
Nor does uncertainty diminish with age,

at most, butterfly wings come, fill the sky
at unguarded moments. No, not the animal:
it's outline he distinguishes, liminal
shape; within that frame, white clouds ride
the blue, as in a Magritte. It hangs there, huge
and frightening, as from a former life,
made of memory, foreboding, rife
with reproach—there washes a deluge
of fear: he is being watched. No god he shapes
in his image; rather, it's a presence
he can sense nearby, a reminiscence
of a form he admires rather than apes—
spirit, in altar smoke. He meditates: again
our dead slide into the American grain ... .

Lower your two eyes' camera. Leave the flame.
Give up, for once, being light and obscure.
Be dark and clear. Consult a book. For sheer
beauty (in Michigan), Monarchs may reign,
while precious stones compete with crystalline blue,
violet, gold tints elsewhere, on a score
of other species; comparisons net more
than ephemeral pleasure, even names. Hue
and cry—yes—for the senses, there is a net
cast wider: an allusion, but a glance, a king
sulphur-yellow, night-blue, in flight: a song,
restraint and symmetry—sound and sight have met.
There, a Monarch shall see his coronation;
crown witness: our performing incarnation.

Watch one alight, wings closed, to perch and rest.
We shout, unheard, dream in chrysalis still;
conquering Monarchs fly over dune and hill,
find flowers, plants: our points to observe them. Blessed,
they are jewels on a golden, sand-built crown.
Now they look like sentries on parapets
of a castle. The spirit who hunts and nets
us all, caught me. How can I pin you down?
We dream of flight, but cannot fly away,
no, not on any airplane, and it burns,
how a butterfly of night-sky blue returns.
Like moths, poets are dust. We leave but stray
evidences of one good, fear-filled flight.
(Never before have I seen such a starry night!)

Consider what we have been. Enchanted souls
given a few hours as reigning kings,
fluttering: worms, upgraded, with powdery wings,
the veins and wing tips burning like live coals;
look in on what we are. Beggars, and more.
Think of Saint Hubert and his Christ-crossed stag,
Dan Webster's devil's moth-soul, or the stage
on which Mark Twain's prince and poor, in pure
terror, switch roles. Caught, we're victim to a scraping
little fool; we freeze, are singed by fire,
impaled—the experts peer, dissect, admire—;
our beauty is our death. There is no escaping
the bottom of a well: you flail in your sleep,
your insect feet lack traction, the walls too steep ... .

Now lie, with trebled heartbeat: morning, power
return—you are a man of blood and loin.
No telling all the sides of Maya's coin.
(Obverse:) Offer up this six-o'clock prayer,
diffident request: Let me see insects streak
(reverse:) against death glass, while suicides
land weightless on the windshield, unharmed. There glides
(converse:) a fine specimen, on Sundays, by the lake—
let no one touch him; within a pebble's throw
(inverse:), resting, we know. And no compassion.
Featherweight spirits have suffered deep concussion
(subverse:); beauty, in silence, in walk, slow, slow—
there is your chase. *So* swing your net, and fly
(adverse:). Your eyes sting. Swallow a pointless cry.

Back in his Venice, Aschenbach was right
to stare, in love, at a spindle-legged boy
who, motionless, could all but stretch and fly,
fuel an old man's shame, his held-back light.
For isn't it in standstill, poise, mature
stride, he stalks princely kill ... the setting sun?
Why shouldn't a king adore his newly-gained son?
Who will ever witness a meteor's
flight, at low altitude, touch-and-go
and, mad on mind-made wings, let out a shout—
I've caught His Majesty! The boy darts out
in dream ... as he once did, thirty years ago.
It is night now. I see no light but him.
The engine is off. My headlights are on low.

2.

Sonnets

Sonnet for Christmas

Triptych, Ferrarese School, c. 1350

On these perpetual holy days the Child
sports a gold-orange swaddling suit, and blue,
the Child-Mother's warm robe circles their chilled
tableaux—two crackled faces, careful glue

alive: we come unstuck. A festive room
yields to the dark of fields, to air and sun,
bare trees; I touch brick walls and hurry home.
An angel humors Mary's little son.

Saints, angels, magi: friends in sorrow, mirth,
watchful, wear haloes. Stores shine. Snow descends.
We celebrate the births of sun and earth;

the year dies out with birth. The haloed fly
by law, deliver kings' gifts as amends
to wondering people for that silent flaw.

After Twelfth Night

Friend, Davy Jones's locker is no place for those deep
brass instruments lost recently in a scuffle
by members of the Houston Symphony,
I said to Sven. If, this late, you wish to lock horns
away to safety, you had better lift the tone arm
in your mind when the closing bars of *Amahl*
fade away, or else put up that new biography of
Teddy Roosevelt. And in general: peace. The avenue
is festive with lights on this rainy night, with
black figures carrying umbrellas silhouetted against
a gas station. They remind you of scurrying
figures in Japanese silkscreens that (as a reviewer
just wrote so well of other works) somehow
satisfy the way the old silents used to.

Reassurances of Summer

For Arabella

Late winter. Cutting wind, the dance
of snowflakes: gone. A pale clear sky
hints at the deep blue of July,
the green and purple elegance

of May. The trees are women dressed
for a wedding. Young couples pass.
Reflected in a car door's glass,
blue eggs lie, fallen from a nest.

In summer, ancient cups shall hold
honey and milk. The melting air
runs down the panes. In pours the gold.

A bird nests in your cupped and bare
hands. A girl kneels in summer grass,
and cuts her boy friend's wintry hair.

Recommendation Statement

24

Miss Argot is a busy-looking student,
but has a tendency to bluff her way.
When I point out the subtleties of poems
her eyes will open wide; she'll say, Oh my,
I hadn't thought of that! But being asked
to speak on images of innocence
in Eliot or Frost, she'll face a task
of eloquence—display of ignorance-
cum-arrogance—almost.
                        She'll blush when I
suggest: it helps to have her piece to say,
and not just take a potshot, hit or miss;
my consolation is a thought the lady
may within the year become a worthy
earpiece to some talker she'll impress.

May Walk

25

Under a solid sky, walking upside down
along a spacious boulevard, I see
lawns lush green as Ireland in November,
flowers, ferns, succulents in unmoving
profusion among stones, as in Japanese gardens.
After the thunderstorm of the night before,
the silent soil growls, but all is fresh;
the water shakes into my face from dense trees
in a deciduous Michigan collection mixed
with evergreens. I walk on and come upon large
tulips, daffodils: jewels in unkempt grass, near
the disheveled white Afros of dandelions, with
fragrant wet green surrounding my gray topcoat,
and the good smell of lightning rising from earth.

Three Ladies

As we ride in early in the morning,
three ladies board the bus and cause a stir.
Their leader wears a coat blacker than mourning
(it's of a plush-soft artificial fur);

their next in line has on a raspberry color;
the third, an antique mustard, here and there faded,
matching a general appearance of pallor.
They look around fifty—not what you would call aged.

They sit in the rear. Frau Mustard spins you yarns,
they never seem to end. Madame Raspberry
measures her speech—it's free of *blank*s and *darn*s;

Mistress Blacker-than-Mourning cuts them off.
Heaven only knows why she disturbs me.
Each time I hear that voice, I'm forced to cough.

Cumae

The ancient lady in the long black dress
approaches, in the whirling afternoon,
the Campidoglio's steps. Under a wan
full moon, in August heat, she is heiress

to another climate. A schoolgirl, breathing
snow-crystal air, the freedom of her poets.
(In front of the Winter Palace, hunger riots
were sabered down, and citizens lay, bleeding.)

Sunlight, Etruscan stone. The walls still stand.
We waited for the Sibyl in a time
Caesars and Czars and language countermand.

"Twin are the gates ...": of doubt, long waiting, towers
where a dictator swept away her home
to open fora for doubly vanished powers.

Mimesis

Twisted metal and glass: look. There they lie
on the shoulder, covered. We'll slowly roll
past. How strange the elementary physics
of movement. Yes: in moving, we must live

clear of touch. Come to full stop, *then* give
an inch. We're basically bashful. I think cynics
are wrong on all the violence. The sole
contact that you may have is with the eye.

What about filmmaking? Actors outfitted
with the lures of the box office: haircut
bloodsmeared, black eyes, dislocated jaws?

All that's hardly for keeps, sir. There are laws.
Blows and kicks must stop short of their target.
Only the lightest contact is permitted.

Dandelion Seedheads

Blown-off dandelion seedheads litter
the tall crabgrass; a squadron of mosquitoes
alight, mean business where soldiers loiter,
talk sweethearts and wives; a billboard misquotes

Thoreau. A broken pane says "Antiques"
in faded letters, gold against an honestly
threadbare shop, with idle boys' antics
copied on the windowpane by a horsefly;

cigarette butts, bloodshot eyes. Microscopy
fails to help me find a phone where an ambulance
should pull up and hustle in all that's uniformed;

I dance on broken glass, deftly miscopy
the seedbed scene. In sorrow, ambivalence,
we trade but glances, half-noticed: uninformed.

On Silence

I mean destructive silence,
not disagreement.
The kind in which you hear
uncalled-for comment,
the whole atmosphere
filling a room
of opinion rampant
in the man's cranium.

At the party he blows smoke,
looks past you, defiles
the premises with silent abuse.
On the expressway he stares
ahead, uses concentration
as his damned excuse.

Detroit Panorama

Beautiful Canada and Michigan
are visible on a clear winter afternoon
from the top of the tallest hotel around.
Belle Isle, railroads, industry. A slow blue
tanker floats on the Detroit River;
on the opposite bank a patient string
of green freight cars waits, with a red caboose.
From inside your brown-tinted glass
elevator shaft, café tower, you see
enormous Ambassador Bridge, screening
a distant marsh of white-smoking factories
and, ninety degrees to the northeast again, on
the Canadian side, a broad avenue, shooting
diagonally into the silver light.

Marigolds

Sunflower seeds stored in small glass jars
in the basement, the quiet of musty walls, thick
black pipes, somewhere a mouse or a raccoon
making pebble or knock-on-wood sounds. Sunlight
enters a slender shaft and dust rises among
cartons, old silver candlesticks, a moldering
how-to-fix-it book, suitcases, shoeboxes,
corrugated paper, dry-cleaning plastic, piles
of bundled *New York Times Magazines*—

                         oh, moving,
Signore, is like suddenly thinking of marigolds,
the newsboy, mailman, of fending off those
too-friendly neighbors, and, on the porch
next door, of an ageing white samoyed
sunning himself in the pale warmth of April.

Postcard

Evocative archival find in an abandoned basement
among old packages, barrels of sawdust, dustwrapped
piles of software, cartons of rusted tools, nails,
auto parts, leftover strips of linoleum and stripping
from a newer building around the block and uphill,
where the business moved but a year ago; while rummaging
here, checking canisters, you breathe fumes,
flay your shin, or have a pipe break loose on your head—
what business has a custodian peering from flammable
cupboards, where no sane city inspector will place
his fire-safety sticker, and rats lie dead, where you
slice darkness like trap bait, where any shapes
will frown but a muttonchop-whiskered Franz Josef
stamp on a Polish town in purple twilight?

Easter Sunday

Some thoughtful choral music on the radio,
a good book in your hand, a quarreling
quadrupletworth of seasonal dialogue
in your mind—what more could satisfy your
breakfast appetite for glaring sunlight,
the image of bright copper utensils
clanging in the neighbors' hidden kitchen,
a view, from an acute angle, of angels
competing in invisibility, completing
in their throats a strenuous job of melody,
heads, arms lifting like branches in a mind
seeing the sun of the Resurrection over a
shy lawn, a young man in a doorway, a lamp
gone out? the fresh bread dough in the oven, risen?

Moonmeal

To Bertolt Brecht
in presumption

What could please Messer Galileo's palate
more than redolent roasted apples,
a young goose or turkey; to fill it,
dressing with thyme and, larger than the subtle
fragrance of dill, the scatter of tiny leaves,
the straight and yet wild vegetable curve of
celery? the orbiting of tiny tomato moons?
Curved, straight, he sees a silver service;
the sun auctions it off, loses on its commission.
Marvelously, light travels in curves, yet straight—
sun to eye, via moon, yet around any corner in
town, of breakfront, it bends. Evidences of light
are the lime, the melon; he longs to record their corona.
However, for that he lacks the proper instrument.

A House All Pictures

The windows vanish; we cannot afford to buy
a Vasarely. Our house is already weighted
with the evening light of framed squares of sky,
and the frame house itself is far too heavily matted.

The walls are literate with the grammar of prints,
the plaster is stalked by the lion of Jerome;
deep in the bricks you see Piranesi's intangible light,
enter the wall and you've entered the city of Rome.

Is home what we hang? It was Gertrude Stein's style
to have her pictures slightly crooked on her walls,
and you cannot peel her Roman emperor smile
from the imperial plaster of a Paris atelier;
the Picassos, oh, her Braques breathed the air of those halls,
an era's gesture entombed in their crackling dismay.

Homage to Edward Hopper

In his landscapes silence is eloquent.
America means standstill: a marquee,
stark markings on a sunlit tenement,
nocturnal barber pole, a cloudlit sea.

A night café, a soundless conversation
behind a huge window of pure curved glass,
a forest road, abandoned service station.
One lonely figure near an underpass.

Clear morning, buildings. In a fourth-floor window
you see a bed, some suitcases: a widow.
Hotel: two men sit staring at a page.

Lampshades and landscapes. Sunlight; composition.
A city square speaks Sunday desolation.
An ancient land lies silent, and is sage.

Celebration

After the venerable scholar had published
his stately series of biographies
of men who did not need them; at his ease,
at last, he thought of how his subjects had perished,

and how reviewers had called him a sorry hack.
Who shall finally judge a life devoted
to lives of men neurotic, ill, demoted,
quarrelsome, and prone to heart attack?

Who should finance a simple marble tablet,
not to Shakespeare—the editor of *Hamlet,*
the man who points, for us, to site and stone?

Yet as his eightieth birthday rolled around,
his fete was thunderous. They broke his ground,
then rose and took him home to die alone.

Rebirth

When the old colonel died, the house stood empty.
His will ordained that all effects be sold,
unpaid-for furniture returned, his gold,
securities redeemed. "Dismiss the sentry.

"Let an unguarded emptiness abide
on either side. Let memory fire a blank.
Once you've wiped out the troops, let weeds march rank,
the soul may indeed have little left to hide."

The devil nursed him to his parting day,
blind soldier, warned him: "If you fail to pay
your exorcist, you may get repossessed";

his creditors foreclosed. He left a skull
empty as a fly's translucent hull,
a gaping home, a corpse without a past.

Lights on Earth

Moonnight to noonsight,
    swamp reed and fern;
frog pond: Walpurgis Night,
    cold silver burn;
burn like an ice globe,
    change forms in sight;
nightwalk: a blind glade,
    starpollen-bright.

Moongleam is sunsent
    softened for eyes,
lumen de lumine,
    spare dream, surprise:
piercepoint in spacenight,
    floodbright to dawnlight,
gold-red, shall rise.

3.

Sesquisonnets

Standalone

43

run your hand
along the aluminum
grating
and tap your

fingers on top
of the fan
it sounds like
endless hollow

steps
approaching
on fire escapes
and metal

rooftops
at the beginning
of a crime film

the narrating
detective's voice
has not yet come on

the blonde near the ledge
has not had a chance
to scream

Barbershop Cavatina

Television blares, scissors snip,
delicate Chinese characters form
on the clean-smelling towel cloth;
magazines on the rack: about machines,
electronics, home repairs, and fishing,
Reader's Digest, and *Saturday Evening Post*
with yet another Norman Rockwell cover.
A mother with three restless small boys waits
her turn. Someone else cuts Chinese ideograms
or painless branches, and barbers talk
as if the music of vegetable gardens,
the latest curved ball in a World Series game,
soldiers and barracks in a dusty summer camp,
and the language of what falls from heads were all.
Outside, in the meantime, the barber pole spins;
someone else comes in; for a second, you see
a running man mirrored in the door.
The minute hand on the wall clock jumps;
cars rush by, you can't see the wheels turn;
I pay, walk out with a clean, well-cropped feeling.
Inside, on the tube, a good show is just starting.

Signs

Do you believe the sun sets on the bright side
of the soul? I said to Sven. Don't be so sure.
When mine got up this morning, there was a huge
circle drawn across the equinox
of memory—exactly thirty-four years
it's been since I first hit these shores.

And, yessir, the stars that secretive morning
were so pale, I thought I was five again, lying
nude under a quartz lamp. I couldn't leave the house
without my radiation-proof umbrella. Once
downtown and in the store, I had to step out of
my worn-out shoes and buy myself a new pair.

And after the salesman had done me his rain dance
I stood there like trees, shining from the feet up,
and felt like the devil, with a club foot. Why was
one shoe about to leave me? The salesman laughed:
Lots of people's left foot's bigger than their right.
Did my mother limp before I was born? He had a point.
When I left the store, Taurus was not to be seen
anywhere across the broad and shining arc; down below,
only a newly-shod wingless bull, if I read the signs.

Sesquisonnet in Purple

Someone wearing a magenta sweater,
face hidden, back turned to me,
hurries by and I murmur, Lady,
all I want is a purple-and-green city bus
to take me home, okay? April—
the air feels cool this clouded

morning, and heavy with the perfume
of fresh lilacs. The city is out
putting up red-white-and-black
traffic signs. Men are pounding.
Patches of lavender: a skirt, a sweater,
pick up colors of apple trees and blossoming

lilac bushes near where I stand, then
a corner patch of fresh flowers—
improbable, as real in my blinking eyes
as is a purple after-image of
the white sun. I see amethysts
sparkling in grass, and in a nearby
shop window, bright with lights and
graphics—rose, orange, brilliant blacks, creams—
a huge ceramic pot of violet glaze.

The One and the Many

Viewing Leonard Baskin's etching "Moses"

This is the Hebrew, the non-Greek. Severe,
jagged black lines around his mouth show
the artist understood. He had let them know:
No scratching, blowing dust, making a clear
image emerge on stone. There was the One
Original, and copying it was a crime.
He could just see them quarrying slabs, in time
doing huge editions, until the One would run
like water between their fingers. He, sculptors' prince
in Egypt, now poor, would teach them to be strong.
(If only *those* two slabs didn't take so long!)
We haven't seen a Baskin "Moses" since

that afternoon, when sunlight etched the eaves,
and doves flew close by, flashing light. We conversed
on miracles in graphics. Colors, first
tomato, barley, sky: Latin weddings, cut
in wood block prints, now multiplied like loaves
around the strident "Moses." And trees held court
for gallery, window, deep blue sky, until
the sun itself lost form and turned to a chill
silver soul among the blazing leaves.

Invention in Wood

All morning the sound of splitting wood.
Transformers on power lines shine silver
near poles; nearer, a brownian motion
of dust specks. Fragrant, fleshy green peppers
lie on a chopping board, while the sun
plays the heliochord: a piece in C major.

Seeing that a frame house bears up under
light on polished oak, I try a dance step.
Termites silently picnic in the woodwork.
A pile of firewood neatly stacked
near a chimney and a dark blue Volkswagen
pose for a picture in a woman's mind

two doors down. I listen to some tree work
resounding in a back garden, behind a spruce.
Boys, men swing out with muffled shouts,
while I, silently ascending the stairs
into my tree house, cannot see a soul,
yet wonder how rafters can manage to muffle
a TV show sounding so thoroughly wooden.
Out on the interchange a semitrailer roars.
A centipede goes down stairs, using its own lane.

A Concert

Lethal rehearsals: two stores burned to the ground,
a nurse raped, seven young students mugged.
Even in the concert version, two are hugged
and fall with a thud. The police are bound
and gagged. Prima donnas are lined up in a bar.
No one knows who the real offenders are.

Someone's notion of an operatic joke?
We get back late. Hardly time for a Coke
and a sandwich, a glance at the papers.
Who needs it? The pay phone in the hall
rings frantically. One more unanswered call.
My eyes smart. The hall lights flicker, like tapers;

we hear a voice. Through a crack in a door
I see a tall young man, seated (about sixteen),
on his face that caught-red-handed look.
A soft voice: "You've done it again, son.
It's those damn shoes. You should be neither heard nor seen."
Puzzled, we look at one another. We hear a lock
snap. Two young girls are led in. We're told to hurry,
as the concert is about to start. Cool night air
blows in raindrops through an open window.

A Little Learning

Over coffee she tells me, whispering, leaning
over: "I've got a closetful of boys.
Each is a utensil to do the cleaning,
all of them were fantastic bargain buys.
Crawford the broom makes you sweeping statements;
Ragtime Randy performs on a cobweb;
Alvin the scrub brush takes to the basement
(he'll bristle and spew at every cracked step)."
There's Samuel, the scholar among her fellows:
he sucks up knowledge like a vacuum sweeper,
restores to Oriental rugs their colors,
and John, the oldest, his four brothers' keeper.

I shudder, hearing that familial account
of the wishful dreams of a childless woman
all dark closets inside, not a shutter
to let in sun and dust. There must abound
lean, locked-in mopheads, love-pretending, cloning
of clowns who'll clean her heart and leave it clutter.
What's all knowledge worth? There's perilous haunt.
I call her; the background hums with cleaning
and boys' voices, a blend of chide and mutter.

Not Available for Comment

God seldom is, but this is to be regretted.
Look at her white, taut, and gentle face,
half-absentminded; she has suffered, I think.
A face cut in, like one of those small panes
in the French door half-open behind us—
with cleanliness. Transparency. Strength. Fragility.

This is it: her first book of poetry,
with her picture on the cover. Once,
remember, when we went out to the cemetery,
you said, for days afterwards you could hear her voice,
irritatingly soft, reading one of the poems.
How did I know she wasn't right here in this room?

Or was it the record player in the garden, a fresh
breeze not turned, for our ears, into those unheard
voices of leaves, whispers? And then you saw:
the face of her mother, whom we had both known well,
reduplicated in mirror and in landscape.
And she is here a mother in her own right, with
three sons, working in the yard, giving us a poem.
Not hearing these four, we ourselves melt
into the picture's flatness. Observe, and be glad.

Undergraduates

"I've never had a teacher like him before!
He shapes me, inside-out, a shivering form;
my woman-flesh turns into living marble;
the colors I hear are an electric storm
at the roots of my whole tall living body.
Two lovers lie, I hear, in a moonlit room.
He wakes up, begins tapping poetic meters
on her back; he writes a reclining poem.
Then he reads us the elegy by Goethe.
The words stick like no rock music ever will,
like burrs to my nerves, to my longing center,
chilling meaning: bone-deep, as I lie still."

"Ours takes this ballad by Heine; he retells
'Die Lorelei.' It's sunset over the Rhine.
Now the girl combs her hair. It's the gold of *gold,*
like rose, *rose, ROSE* again, shining syllables,
an endless conversation in your mind.
The 'Lorelei' is an old movie retold,
he says, a tale relived; it makes the pulse
in your ankles quicken. His voice is gentle and kind;
I'm clasped firm in a friend's arms, hot and cold!"

State of the Art

Coffee, sugar, tobacco—
these were the three the old seminarian
wanted from home (on screaming winter
mornings, up at four by candlelight,
because the prince said so), and when he did
receive them, he was ready to share all three, but
who had ever heard of a coffee machine (besides,
they stole the sugar for the stables)? And
the now well-tempered seminarian would
gladly have played preludes on an equally
evenly-tuned clavecin, but never in his life
would he be privileged to finger one,

until doddering old age brought him to a river,
and they locked him into his round tower,
there to contemplate the mystery of flow
and standstill, for forty more silent years.
So he contented himself with the tobacco
and, filling his pipe early with melodies,
he played clear clouds into sunlight, to his
barracks-mates who had come for a visit,
heard, and coughed with gray incomprehension.

Imagined

Conversation with the shy teenage daughter
of the lady running the rapid copy shop:

"Don't be bored, child. There's too much beauty,
too much to do. Take little old me.
When I was your age, I thought I wanted
to become a composer. And, yes, at night
I heard tunes I thought were my own,
but turned out to be pale echoes
of a different place, another time.

"Then, one night, I heard the 'Lullaby of Broadway,'
woke to the tune of clinking milk bottles,
and never again put pen to music paper.

"By then I knew—oh child, I had learned
you can't copy Mozart, any more than
you can xerox yourself. You can't; so don't."

I don't remember whether I thought all this
in the shop, or rehearsed it, once outside again;
never a word of it did I say out loud.
All the young lady did was bring coffee,
then stare up at the pious monk in the poster
announcing: "The Miracle Machine Has Arrived!"

It Makes Waves, Mr. George

Says the smiling travel agent,
praising the artificial pool
of a spa up in the Buda hills.
I know. I knew it as a kid,

and have made waves myself since.
Sunny Chicago,
drawbridge, Tribune Tower,
Sears, Wrigley Building,

over the blue of lake and river,
make waves, but south of the Loop
your steps are crunchier,

your eyes get caught on
sunlight reflected off broken bottles,
green waves—
oh this is Carl Sandburg country,

where no one makes waves;
ten boarded-up windows
and a good-smelling bar

make a tiny wave. I wave back.
I know it does, Mr. Tomkins.
Been making them myself ever since.

Darryl and Girolamo, or The Search for Truth

Centuries separate them; no accident
of place or swimming time that far outswims
the self in search of self can nudge the hand
of a clock, shift global axis, to change the whims
of the expanding universe, and cause
these two to stop, stand face to face, inform
themselves of burdensome resemblance. Close,
they would acknowledge distance, yet confirm
the law that wisdom and incomprehension,
if mutually invalid, cannot shut out
reminiscence in style, in the mansion—
delivery, in measured phrase or shout.

Shared iconographies of brutal waking
date both: hairshirt; a polio patient's crutch.
Each bears his by an old act: confirmation,
orb and scepter of office. Let no weakling
up on his trends, deride the agonic clutch
at open book, the classic sense of mission.
Savonarola, Schultz, in entente staking
integrity on utterance, now catch
themselves, mid-sermon, to risk unimpaired motion.

Piazza

One glance will do: Siena, City Hall,
podestà, pride—immense on a four-by-four
Kodachrome snapshot. Think of an honor roll
of heretics, doomed in the public square.
Not that it matters whether Siena itself
was ever party to such brutal acts,
in confrontation of Ghibelline with Guelf.
Not that facts matter. I have no lease on facts,
those slum tenements of our governance,
in whose alleyways wisdom runs amok.
What fascinates is open space: distance
around a fine old building. The eye is struck.

Space is what good buildings are here to sculpt.
The palazzo uses heretics'
thinking bodies: we dull to ash, then bulk,
expand and fill the unsuspecting air
as helium fills balloons. The buildings fix
stereometric clarities, and bare,
the tower, fountain, walls command your touch.
How much spirit-combustion it must take
to shape one perfect forum, I muse. How much? ... .

Scandinavian Snapshots

Speed and graphic distortion of language,
and paths, once familiar, now blurred,
give you the illusion of clarity
and the unhoped-for brilliance of midnight:

on a train, past a torchlit restaurant,
before a crowd, far out, as on the great ice,
yet near, as in a crowded telephone booth,
the walk goes on, as in a Bergman screen play.

At a busy traffic intersection,
little green men carrying Hans Christian
Andersen's umbrella walk in the lights.
The Tivoli Gardens. A highrise. *SAS.*

And a city, a kingdom of golden crowns
and angels above the gates, royalty
invisible above the waters surrounding

streets that float in mauve-brown twilight.
Strindberg, posing as Prometheus, in the park;
and then, goodbye. To friends, a century gone.

Hamlet nowhere in his castle. The sun
at Helsingør also sets: lighthouses, twin ports;
Denmark's sweet-smelling roses, the rust of blood.

.

Greetings from Israel

In a land of hot sun and sweet spring air
evergreens grow as if they needed to
populate the yearning corridors
between the gold of sky and the blue of earth
with groves planted thickly, with palms of peace.
In Israel, o postcard-receiving Son of Zion,
not only is it true that all daily business
should begin and conclude on the word *Shalom,*
"Peace be with you"; "And with you too be peace";
more: every orange tree, each ancient stone,
golden like earth, like marble of recent quarry,
is a firm greeting—we ask you imagine it.

The Arab guard behind the barbed-wire peace fence
guards his carbine, lest his lips move and the alien
blood of language issue forth. The walls don't move
—they've stood there, no comment, these two thousand years—
but road signs are iconographies of progress,
and trees, tall, graceful as daughters near wells,
are dark and moving as a column of serious soldiers,
men and women together, off to the desert,
to protect the trees, their rigorously ordered lives.

Sequoias

North of San Francisco, where the city
neatly changes back into nature again,
the great ancient sequoia forests live,
dark brownish-red against the peaceful sky—
trees so large around, you fail to move
your mind to analogy with columns, slain
Titans—no. Only trees of like integrity

can hope to do them justice. Along that route
the peaceful sequoias create another world:
unheard-of landscapes, a grand canyon inverted,
armies of lumbermen tall as the sky,
plants reaching for the sun, highrises herded
together, though no skyscraper would hold
our imaginations, stay stout

to its core, like a sequoia redwood tree.
We've visited that forest, having been told:
Drive across the vermillion Golden Gate
alone, on a Sunday morning in early March,
and there they'll be. And that whole part of the state
is sequoia country; south of town too the gold
redwoods range on southward: ancient, noble, free.

West Virginia

Children of mountains, descent into hell is easy,
it's coming up back the other side that's hopeless.
Pushing the toothpaste back into the tube
is a parlor game by comparison. But try it.
Unrob a bank; make a ripe orange green again.
Separate the coffee from the cream.

There's a bedeviled fool, trying to rewrinkle
animals he had ironed on the highway.
Here is one whose career it's been to make
trees out of books. Whole libraries turn forests.
Farther off, junkyards of automobile bodies
become mountains carrying virgin ore.

A kind of recycling; some make it work.
Unbetraying a wronged associate's trust;
trying not to listen in on a meeting
that doesn't concern them (it does); patching
a hole they busted in immemorial air.
I have to drive on through. Let me know
how it goes for the ones who reattain birth,
reenter Mining Mother Earth, successfully turn
blurted-out words back into holy secrets.

Looking for Ezra Pound in Venice

For O. S. P.

We looked in at the Café Florian,
hoping for a shutter's glance at that Homeric head
under the slender panel oils, mirrors; ahead,
in darkness: empty rooms. Footsore, touring on
through sun-etched arcades, we sailed a yellow, sound-
less sea of wire chairs and tables, saw an ounce
of an old man in a black hat (he threw a lance
at us; I gripped your arm: "That's Ezra Pound!");
we came to the doorstep of impatient waters
("or is it that old man, leaning against the lamppost?");
the world, that day, was veering away from its own coast,
murmuring canto fragments in crumbling corners.

You, influential Sire, who succeed
Confucian Doges on a lagoon of dreams,
help our air walk, lift to a level of sight
our citymad myth, stoneharnessed hippogryph
(now both eyes fix you from a photograph),
over the sustaining sea, our blurred, worshipful light.
Stravinsky held us so, your strange confrère who, reaping
the joy and terror of Venice, came, already sleeping
his canticle of rage into our foundering night.

4.

Doublesonnets

Voices

Bone tissue grows in a sleeping child.
Electrons whirl in the bedroom wall.
I look into the bathroom mirror.
The peonies in my yard open.
Fog burns off by noon.
An engaged couple smile in a jewelry ad.
Your next-door neighbor talks to you in his dream.
A foetus differentiates.

A statue at Chartres smiles at Rodin.
Tin soldiers converse.
A star falls in August.
Milk sours in the refrigerator.
Marine life evolves.
Leaves turn color in September.
A deaf boy listens to Beethoven.
The Kamakura Buddha meditates.

Prices rise.
A choir sings on a record album cover.
The sun is eclipsed by the moon.
Morning light moves over the peaks of the Sierras.
Earth turns in orbit.
Truman holds up "Dewey Defeats Truman."

The man in the moon gives an interview.
Rome falls.
A luminous chalice relieves two silhouetted profiles.
A reflected bridge forms a perfect circle.
An apostle in a Masaccio painting shouts something.
My unforgotten dead sing in the center of the sun.

Cadillacs

A streak of Cadillacs created brown and gold,
driven by blacks and decorated with a quilt
of multicolored, lovely fresh carnations—white,
pink, blue, and lilac, green, and all the subtle hues,
pulled down the gleaming boulevard and honked aloud,
and honked and honked; a fine parade: exuberant
"Just Married" cars were putting on a caroling
procession, singing horns, a choral festival
of blues and negro golds, the joy of Africa-
America, in summertime, an August sun's
December snowdrift's worth. The wilder caroling
not letting up at traffic lights, or round the bend,
the carhorn-musicale now fades; now fresh reserves
renew a music fiercer than the song before,
a ricercare, passacaglia, ritornell
of *hoot-hoot, taa-taa;* purple, silver carhorn tones
pursue you unawares right down the avenue,
weddings in light brown dreams, in old daguerrotypes,
unlikely music, late in summer's faded eye—
brown, gold, indeed. ... How come the fleet of Cadillacs
have taken to their heels? The hotel loggia there,
relaxing in the gold sun of late afternoon,
swallowed them up. But now the carhorn-choir resounds,
if anything, more fiercely and more deafening
than yelping friends before them. Are they vengefully
pursuing me: a squadron of Eumenides,
for ancient, summoned guilt, for incest, patricide,
for usurpation, crimes?
                    Oh, no: my lights were on.

Alexandrite, or Jeweler in Purgatory

Yes, friend, I know it's dark. No, I am no one new.
You are meeting your old jeweler from Chicago.
Had my shop on uptown Michigan Avenue,
remember? There, last fall, I saw you in my window,
your face engraved with pain. A stone, an alexandrite
hung from a silver chain, lay there, threw violet fire.
Throwing a glance at me, you mounted its deep light
and stole it in your mind, for stone-mirrored desire

to dwell in stones and glow. I credit you for sending
not one false spark at first. Yet an unjeweled hand
reached from inside your mind (you had begun descending);
a brief struggle ensued for quasi-contraband.
The alexandrite stayed; its firelight was bent.
I saw you walk and sink where evening traffic crawled.
A clumsy city bus; police wrote "Accident."
Teeth of my eyes, clairvoyant jewelstones, left you mauled.

Now in the fire of suns, stoneburner as before,
I enter this bright red tunnel before you, seer
seeing the led, not blind. Memory locks my store.
I'm blinded wondering if metropolitan traffic
laws were stricter up there than laws of downtowns here;
whether, when outlaws die, their earthly lives shine classic,
chiseled in stone; whether, when modern legends pale,
death sends a sign, from stone, of vengeance hard and clear,
releasing inner light that bends, yet cannot fail.
One stone we both have held gave us temerity
to face the cleansing flames, repent; to hold off fear.
Our question has since stayed one of sincerity.

Summer Camp

Don't look back through the screen—a movement, vanishing—
it's dark in there. At most you'll see a pale moth
between the bedspread and the white cotton lining
of the drapes. Now it's gone. No, she is not loath
to talk to you. But take it easy. You frightened
the dickens out of her, that's all. Too demanding.
Press yourself. Like a book cover, you'll straighten.
You'll see her tonight. Show some understanding.

Can't see inside you, either. There, large, moldered
coins, old stamps, scrapbooks, lie in a cave. First
you squint as you emerge from chaos; then, maybe, fold
securities deep in pockets, feel neatness. Thirst,
pride: those come later. Sepia portraits move
and speak in your dreams, near dawn; playing bass, you keep
time so precise, you don't even know it. A velvet glove—
press, the strings, to silence them. You start from your sleep.

Look out to the lake, the sun, whose friendly fire
kindles water a thousandfold, and does not burn.
Hold out your left hand. Now the right. A bit farther,
line them up: they overlap. Not duplicates, not twins—
they're opposites. A shorted wire: we touch, we're caught,
drawn inward, driven, need to break out. Plain sense
tells us, though: whatever we do—kick a ball, paint
the garage—a one-person audience may gather, applaud;
we perform, take our bows, maybe, and no sweet restraint
holds back long years when high-strung hours shall play
their duo on you both. Yet you will want it, whole.
Now go on. Just for a while longer. Be a boy.

Advice to Someone's Daughter

"He licked me on the face, and it hurt."
Of course it did, dear. Gratitude for
an armful of affection does not change
the furniture of feeling. Tiny bumps shine
on his tongue, parallel matching, colluding
occlusions, fittings, in his mouth (I hear
a man's voice, a buzz-saw going in the yard);
fine, sharp-edged growths, coming close, close,

points that surface thank you's ride on. Who knows?
The next time you feed him, he may even eat you
without your as much as noticing he was
(I know you love him: watch it) saying Thanks.
Do you remember that picture in the paper
of a wealthy man who had bought one at auction
(it was described as hollow, and of light brass),
and how glad he was he would never have to feed it?

"But I have to feed *mine?* And how am I to do it
at arm's length, where he runs and plays?"
Yes, dear, I know. Where the bulk that we ourselves
are, remains. Where no one can swallow,
hoof and sod, specious worry about our being
out there but a toothsome form, constant,
raw, redolent with vegetable spirits
unmoved by hunger. Afraid, yet knowing full well
others can't swallow us. Stubbornly we stand
our ground, with a quiet double-dare; then we fret.
Go on back out there. Offer him a carrot,
extended on the palm of your hand.

Theseus in the Prairie Grass

This, Ariadne, is what a labyrinth should be!
Back when I was just drawing my sword
and wondering why, old Bullhead said, "My boy,
you'll have no rest once you're through with me.
You'll leave this labyrinth, this land, and go
on a journey, and not stop until you've fathered
antique swords sheathed in a rough people's minds.
Until you've arrived at what all flesh shall know."

Is then all flesh sea or desert? Could that blade
still fail to strike its proper metallic chord,
while I remain in the presence of a sun that
bakes and consumes its self-devouring self
in memory? Do we still cut our fingers on thread
and collide with creatures we cannot see?
What did Bull mean? Can thought, like swords, be honed
after dulling crossings over rust, sea, and wind?

Oh, how the grass whispers above my head
as, desperately, I walk and turn and turn,
finding neither a path out to the road
nor a footpath to lead me truly outward,
back to our labyrinth: to bullhall,
plinth, sword, abandoned Ariadne weeping.
How bullheaded all our ancient kill
seems now! At night, when I can but scan the sky
and descry the Constellation of the Bull,
I thank our poets who sang tauromachies, then
wait for Minotaur to identify other entangled
uncles asking to be dispatched with skill.

Enchanted Prince

This is no time for *Arabian Nights* tales,
of a prince: he was kept under lock and key
by an uncle (who wanted power at last,
and money, and was forsooth a bastard).
The prisoner sang, attracted travelers,
shocking them by what was plain to see—
a child enchanted. Human above the waist,
below he was modeled in pure alabaster.

Nor for martyr legends: a Jesuit priest
caught in Cappadocia is given a choice.
Does he wish to die like his brothers-in-awe,
or, might he think himself "more-than-equal"?
He answers, In Christ we want the genuine test
of love: that makes us equals. Hearing that voice,
the heathen place him in a press and saw
a sagittal section, beginning at the skull.

Believe me, Sister, it's not to entertain us
at a time like this with bone-crushing stories,
with Father sitting spellbound in the saddest
enchantment, waist down: turned stone, like a tomb,
that I tell this. He churned inside that accident,
and the Talespinner's wheel went spinning with it.

When last I slammed on the brakes, it was painless.
This season we cannot choose among our horrors
humbly enough. Isn't instant sawdust
lighter than this royal vegetable doom of
stiffening, rolling? Tell them I only meant
to cheer Father, once it's all right to visit.

Projects

One peers over test tubes, samples soils;
one sits with a stack of vouchers and signs.
A third stares at just-delivered designs
for a city. A fourth sees huge brass coils
emit sparks each the size of a man—
the engineers, the giant project monies, loom
menacing as cyclotrons in a room
no man will enter: neither dare nor can.

Another secret: how noted the place is
for projects the students themselves mastermind.
The giant yo-yo the seniors have designed,
built, and installed as their honors thesis.
See it mounted on their one-hundred-meter
science tower there? You'll never get bored
watching it go up-down on its nylon cord.
They operate it by a small electric motor.

Yes. Those are bicycle wheels, not car tires.
Up and down it goes. Should outsiders compare
what professors do in their marble towers
with yo-yos, I'll point out: the institution fires
the radical professor from the very classroom,
and hires the bum. The true-blue drone retires,
yet comes in and keeps his office door ajar,
just enough to slip out the bicycle wheel.
He will let not a one administrator bar
the kids who run the shops. And I say one admires
the skill and nerve. Already you hear
that seven-foot frisbee whirring through the foyers.

Man with Birds

The man relaxes on a snow-covered bench
before his big-city apartment's door.
Fungi emitting a faint, piercing stench
invisibly infect the winter air;
bare trees rise just behind the benches, stand
guard as he feeds birds at his third-floor window.
The man rises, takes walks, mails contraband.
No citizen's life is less invisible

than each crushing step he takes, no one's stronger.
His books threaten to topple over him
and his. (There have been phone calls.) He is no watcher
for falling rocks. He has been there, and sobering
as the wine bottle he uses to decorate
his table, is the life he at one time bled,
its sting and stench. He will not meditate
compromise. He'll sit, though on a sled.

He will not leave. It's one thing to have both eyes
sound—to see all. He has been there, and knows
the spirit's waterland, and how it lies
drained of its lies. The city where he lives
is warm with icy monuments, and cold
with coal braziers on which, all over, lives
are raked; where every tortured spirit glows
with longing memory of one no sighs,
no nosing for the fungi in the snows
will resurrect. He has returned. Now he sows
sunflower seeds on snow. Unless he tries,
no one will feed the pigeons, feed the crows.

Taxi Ride

Remembering December 26, 1972

We're losing altitude: the streets,
warehouses, traffic, overpass
approach ("We ask you pull your seats
upright!"); the sky is overcast,

morose. A spacious taxicab
rolls us past fields of spirits killed
in rail yards, ship docks, factories,
slum tenements (half of them sealed);

the riverfront, gray bridges, hold
the skyline distant, black and cold.
A winter night without a moon;
apartment buildings, plain and vast;
you rouse me: "Flags are down half-mast—
Truman just died." That afternoon

you'd heard it on the radio.
I hold my breath, try keeping still,
an acid past—you never know
how much of it is safe to spill:

"I respected the sinewy, tough
old President. Hats off, and low,
to any mortal big enough
to tell MacArthur where to go."

It's out the door; too late to run.
We know we'll pay a tidy sum
when lights go on and thoughts are read;
with lampposts passing in review,
a cab slides down First Avenue
reluctantly among the dead.

Tombs near Austin

Brakeing to sixty-five, so that the trees
on the horizon could finally pass us,
Belle said, That bulbous, windowless building
is the Lyndon B. Johnson Memorial Library.
I don't wish to see it, I answered quietly,
looking out the window at a white space module.
She stared at me from the wheel; her eyes were saying,
Recite me no poems; just look. And I sat there, seeing

in the graffiti of the New York subway
the artist still quote Plotinus and admonish
the President to get out of the Blue Room
before all rooms shine the yellow of blood.
Passing lights on the station's tiled walls
were speech, and silence the roar of the gray
train as it pulled in, its illegible fat
graffiti resembling tattoos on circus freaks.

Like winter's dun leaves, it was too gray a day to see
tall evergreens standing out in contrast
over the red of our embarrassed silence.
But a blue-gold sky unfurling on Memorial Day
would show us a review stand groaning under
the weight of all those names engraved in marble.
Let's hurry. Back home, the phone may ring again.
The President has only recently ordered
the bombing of a tiny jewel palace
in the capital city of a kingdom buried
somewhere deep in a rain forest of our minds.

Khmer kings stir in their tombs.

Your Friend and Mine

There are secrets we cannot give away
even to each other. You say you caught your friend
about to turn into a sycamore tree.
Earlier, he had been a mountain lion,
a pickup truck, a beggar's cup, a leopard,
a rosy palace in Jaipur; in quick turns,
all ten incarnations of the god Vishnu—at last,
a drop of vodka on a hissing stone.

Metempsychosis is not the issue. You object
that I have never met my best friend, either.
True. But take a look at this photograph.
Last night, too, I saw his Louis XIV
hat and cape and scepter-shaped umbrella
on the hall coat tree (only he goes around
in period costume). Upstairs later, I heard
his voice behind closed doors: clear talk and laughter.

You ask, What is symbolic of a friend?
How do you know he is there when you need him?
Is he supposed to be a god? a road?
Or should he manifest his presence in some sign,
however modest, that you are familiar with?
You say, Mere signs won't do. I have his fingerprints
memorized. He appears on all the TV networks,
and they are now making a film on his life.
Almost every day I receive mail from him.
Nights, when I hear my name called and dare not move,
he comes and throws pebbles against my window.
His steps come close, stop, start, and die away.

Rest on the Flight to Egypt

How was I to know in the plush bar and
theater of seats in our Boeing 747
that Alitalia Flight 1509,
out of New York, destination Cairo,
would not be stopping in Rome, after all?
"There will be one stop, Ladies and Gentlemen—
on the Azores. You'll have a chance to deplane
and breathe Columbus's famous ocean air."

You could do worse than be detoured by night.
On this first descent of the journey they'd shown us
slides of Old Masters at the Prado,
and of antiquities at the Cairo Museum.
I recall letting the stewardess know
how pleased I was that for once it wasn't
star-war movies or jazz-on-the-rocks.
She blushed, shrugged, and walked off in a huff.

Obediently I breathed their island air,
and amused myself with the "Terra nostra" signs.
An old Portuguese porter who looked for all the world
like Toscanini's grandfather, brought me some water.
I said to him "Grazie," and as he grinned I recalled
a woman I once met in another insular night,

seated on a donkey, an infant in her arms,
and a white-haired Italian reaching her a drink.
Light from an ocean of green came in on them
at the edges of a clearing where they had landed
on the sloping terrain of memory, they too
at sea and yet at peace, illumined somehow.

Grief

He cackled aloud at his mother's funeral
—I saw it—then went home and entertained lone grief
for a month. A drama critic, he plies his chief
trade at night; pity and fear in general
he leaves to the school books. The audience can howl,
shed tears, or laugh; he'll sit through that Shaw performance
pokerfaced and angry. What he finds enormous
are the cold, blank stares you meet in the windswept hall

afterwards. The flask of sympathy everyone bottles
until just curtain. That no one identifies
with Joan's fires; that our howls and *Ohs* are lies.
Catharsis had best be measured in aristotles,
he once wrote, as is tension in volts. That it's not life,
any more than someone's funeral is your death;
than tears are properly shed to Beckett, or to Brecht.
That faces long only in public flaunt belief.

I say he is right. Today I had to attend
a funeral, prior to which there had been a mixup
of corpses. A thoroughly embarrassing event.
Of heads piously bowed in grief there was no need.
But they had to have the correct body brought in
before the burial service itself could proceed,
before the poor rabbi could even pronounce
the sacred syllables that the solemn occasion
under normally aggrieved circumstances demands.
At last there emerged reasonable mimicry
of sorrow. I dared hardly cast up a secret glance
for fear I'd face a roomful of death mask and irony.

I can't agree with you. That funeral
you tell of was a mask of death rehearsed.
Consider: for the first body, a hearse
was never hired. A trumped-up honor roll
of recently deceased old folks now serves
as a roster of the misidentified.
Morticians laugh; the local paper lied.
All to retune the congregation's nerves.

What you imply is that, if we respond
to good theater—Ionesco, say—with tears,
because belief compels us, up in those tiers,
and then put on the freeze enroute to the *grand
escalier,* we've lied. That the ancient and royal
institution brings us a structured art
of the mind; that an interfering heart
can bilk the best of nights. That the rest is spoil.

Could it be that *Catharsis* is but the name
for a broom with which we sweep the hippodrome
of mimesis? that if, snuffed choked, we sigh
at measured speech, at masks that represent
the politics of mean nobility,
then agent and reagent join in a family
of played-out semblance? that carefully dosed depiction
of tears is meant to match the fleshed-out fiction
it honors? that, actors in our element,
at public funerals we but see the stare,
the mask that the critic-poet shall nightly wear,
the truth to which our pieties must give the daily lie?

Prometheus

He fired God and plagiarized the fire,
and published all the flames in the hottest how-to
book of the season. He'd teach people to cook,
make locks and fittings, manufacture armor,
help the consumer if it cost him his game,
cordial relations with Nobodaddy Kronos
up there, and all his foolhill-clinging cronies.
He'd had enough of myths. A love-starved groom
will have his bride; a people would not bide
their precious time and live like savages.
Why couldn't they even fry sausages
and eggs for breakfast? What was there left to forbid?
Then Kronos' police and their sadistic humor ... .
An eagle would be sent to: *de-liver* him,
unless ... . It was a nerveless part of a man,
didn't they know? He relaxed with his Homer.

All that took place three thousand years ago.
He had since retired. His "Firehammer School"
prospered at first, but students graduated
to pyrotactics, murderous up-and-go.
Brilliant glass pears, soft-colored tubes at night
lit up; then, over the sea, one afternoon
in August, he felt the stars, sun, and moon
fuse and collapse. He saw a horrible light,
a giant mushroom rising, a tidal-wave-shaped
fortress. Their latest patent. ... He recanted, humbled;
in a show of power, two cities were showered
with mushroom fire, and God was reinstated.

Rhineland Gothic

Tourism, archaeology, and war
have raised the blackened stone to half the height
of heaven; twin towers hollow to the sore
sight, infrangible this side the light
of sun-moon thinkers, builders in belief
now fragmentary as collapsing age,
of stonemason and sculptor, stubborn, brief-
lived, wild-controlled as chisel, ink-penned page,

as line and filigree, as minds intent
on peace and power, on millennia
of knowledge, solid as the sonorous Mass,
unmoved in change—exploding *Gloria—;*
on polymorphous pillars made to bear
trajectories of stone that meet in vault,
on clerestory and ceiling, transept, choir,
where balanced weight and counterweight shall halt,

on Gothic insects spinning in that loft,
Platonic numbers: volume, mass, and line,
footsteps of giants who worked here once, and left,
still flooded with the Light of the Divine
where grandfathers worked gargoyle and roof tile,
mortared in much too late a century,
in Wilhelminian Gothic revival,
imitative yet seamless mimicry—
so it stands, and stranger, in Cologne,
by riverbank, one fragile colony,
near the great silent ship, unmoved, of stone,
by cruising glance and rifling memory.

Moiré

Moiré is the visual effect created
   when one closely striated or hatched
pattern: a car grill, a fence, a surface of silk,
   coincides with another. Movement
results, as when, given that both surfaces
   are physically at a perfect standstill,
you move your head or entire upper torso.
   The substance is here; in circles, the lines elude you.

It is not the effect you obtain when you take a clean
   porcelain cup in a brightly lit room,
and, holding the cup under the light, you rotate it,
   and you see delicate paraboloid
figures of light. Pure, light-white, they come at you, vanish,
   depending on which way you tilt the cup.
Magical curves you can draw with pencil and ruler.
   A mood iridescent *and* hyperbolic is Moiré.

What is not Moiré is patterns of light—white clouds
   on a still, clear day, when, high up and looking
down on them, you try hard not to descry a face,
   for to see faces when your own face looks back on you,
mirrored, serious, out of the small round window
   near your seat, would make too much a counterpoint
of shapes. There, one had hoped to find an expressive
   landscape of light: grid lines, brown and green land,
land and light, far from car grills and screens, but not far
   from the source of that light which does still imprint
its intelligence on a curved interior space.
   Form is its clarity, the whiteness in a cup, of a face,
knowing the light curve is its model, sculpting a living form.

To an Old Teacher

In memoriam W. H. B.

Congratulations on your walks, deep green
summers down south, your mown golf links, a land
where streets of empty model homes begin
while, forty years fulfilled, your work shall end;
on showing younger men a golden year
irradiated ultraviolet:
the ghosts of texts detected, outlined clear
against old, bungling scribes' defilement.

We heard your classic tale of death by air—
a great library bombed. Its prefect saw
a Medici contessa's locks of hair
preserved, while the scrolls of the Roman law
lay, burned to ash on broken marble floors.
Of how he then gave thanks for wall and limb,
let in fresh air through gaping corridors,
appealed to men, to tall gilt seraphim.

Through panes of glass absorbing solar heat
where earth again inclines to warmth of days
and winter's green-and-black-and-white recedes,
we see your gold-white hair, your figure, bent;
trajectories: traced by a tiny sphere,
and by your search for vowel and consonant.
And on that lesser and greater curve, so white
that to your eyes it's indiscriminate,
nature has written in ultraviolet light
your valediction: more than we all perceive.
Forgive our young rage; watch our silent fall,
our sky-traced path, the ball you will not retrieve.

83

A Voice from the Deep

Take them as a voice from the deep: that summer's riches,
the meadow, the sagebrush, the logs we felled,
the ant colonies, and for each, a cornucopia of
local legends stored in plain and mountain.
Yet it felt late when the air grew hot,
the mules sickened, the help became impatient,
and over beer and poker we missed our wives and kids.
The mails were brought only as far as the camp.

The land itself has its consolations. In the canyon
a mountain-fresh stream, flowers, even some garnet!
And we left with a hoard after the stones had
fairly begged us to pick them up and polish them.
Sudden fatigue overtook me. Closing my eyes
a second, and feeling the world revolve, I almost fell;
you caught me, handed me a canteen. We then saw
from the distance a great sandstone cathedral, one

we could never have picked out had we not worked
inside one like it, some summers ago. To know ourselves
from our surroundings is, I hear, knowledge
(it takes the haptic sense, acutely developed);
to understand feeling surfaces (touch your hand—
this stone—your hand once again) and yet to ask,
is to head for a great interior. It was time.
We gathered our tools, provisions, packed the animals,
synchronized watches at noon, and turned back to town,
only half-satisfied with the silo-studded prairies
of our minds: studious, rearing words, locating,
mapping, sketching the land's overgrown faces.

5.

King versus Knave

experiar quid concedatur in illos,
quorum Flaminia tegitur cinis atque Latina.
—Juvenal

King versus Knave

Receding hairline, slack jaw, double chin,
moist lips, watering eyes—the man must talk;
a young Englishman faces him: good stalk,
strong trap, fat kill. Chagrin, a hollow grin
over the old king's face. An overdue
accounting: for faded crimes, by a dissident
from credible conscience; for rubble, sentiment
(in a sundown, touchdown, showdown interview)
he fled when glass was smashed, steel forced, when halls
were haunted with the echoes of old saws,
of twisted sound, invisible mêlée;
when wisdom, counsel, loyalty went sour,
with power bursting open, a festering sore;
tears stung—a maudlin speech, a liftaway ... .

His look is three-dimensional and warm,
one viewer reflects; the silver screen is cold;
there's sound. The show is on. He hears of gold
days in a city of green, an inkling town
of neoclassic haze; of camp-roughing days
in mountains: royal spring, a cabin, staff
meetings *sur l'herbe;* of boast, innuendo, bluff
overlooking a bluff; of tulips, skies,
red, blue as sea-sky depths of purity
in hot springtime. Standing on a balcony,
the king fires his closest aide. A swarm—
bees, in the gold blue. At last he understands:
he has lost it all. He wrings his trembling hands,
his face an old clock ringing with alarm,

and why? Just what had happened? Why should a man,
if he still *is* a man, allow himself
to be cornered and made to talk for pelf?
Memory glazes the viewer's absent, wan
face—other times and kings—when talk was as scarce
as it is abundant now. The grownups
sat around the dinner table. Glass, cups,
silver, napkins: silence. Insult, a farce—
not a world meant for children. He was deaf, dumb
(or else the door was shut). A radio
was on, a bit of an oratorio;
more likely, hit tunes. His allowance! A dime
is all he would ask for, just as an excuse. ...
Laughter, sudden uproar—oh, what's the use,

again, not a word about his emperor.
A murdered archduke? Now that was man talk. A shot
is all he ever heard mentioned. Then a hot
bath *(it's time, young man!),* and in bed a store
of reflection. Saint Stephen, the first king,
then Anjou, Habsburg. Tribal helmet, crown,
gifts; heavy jeweled tourniquet, a frown
on a Holy Roman brow, the metallic ring
of authority—no. A postage stamp?
An old engraving in a book? To revamp
the Byzantine court takes more than coins and laces.
MacBird will never be crowned Macbeth. We know
genuine grief, reading but eyes. Let him go
back to black-silver faces, a *Mass* by Lassus.

What do we leave? Precept to other earths
on how to orbit suns in mid-career?
The sound is on. You may not wish to hear
how two men speak, in unison; a curse
of glossolalia, cacophonic speech
grabs both by the lapel. Each interrupts
the other; the viewer is collared. Two pups
yelp this way in the back yard, pooch
rhetoric, dogged debate (it's the bark
aims for the jugular; no bite). No answer,
only questions. Alchemist, necromancer
can point to tube, alembic. In pitch dark
you cannot point to dawn for a blinded brother.
Shredded light descends. You hear a stutter,

then the announcer. Surgeon, scalpel thyself.
Viewer thinks: let all the millions now watching
try to explain, point fingers, yes, splotch ink
on reputations black as snow, and shelve
the book of judgment. A suit thus tailor-made
cannot resist filing or trying on
(double-breasted embarrassment, my son—
the courts will mothproof it, in the sun). Brocade
fades, the delicate gold threads run brown;
the man who clothed the highest office is down
(I close the door: His Majesty is undressing
where his mirror of self-virility
fails to reflect—what price duplicity?
The clothes are there. It's the emperor who is missing!).

Like bees, air buzzing, sunlight on beds of flowers.
Once, there was self-assurance, joking, laughter.
Viewer hears an anecdote: "My elder daughter
once told me, 'Dad, those white, mysterious doors
open onto a room with shape and logic.
Oval floor, wall ... . Bird, crocodile, or snake,
whatever the birth, it's here ideas take
form, action is hatched.' (Soft stir, a sound of lodging—
eggshells cracking.) We left the double door
open to a summer recital of air,
to bird habitats of a trim June garden,
to deep green, acacias, roses, the gravel walk,
a metal garden table—to seclusion, and work."
And that was a whole year before the Pardon.

*

What had he done that was so terribly wrong?
A call, a lengthy tape, a telling brown-
out; wrong address; hand to a slipping crown.
They'd roar, fourscore and seven million strong,
and he'd reply, care not a mildewed Lincoln cent,
let them prove, while unreeling his record, or try,
once they found out what he knew (some would fry
in their own fat)—*he was, would be innocent.*
Case dismissed? What was damaging? To whom?
There were, after all, signs. A smoking pistol ... ;
red faces. Money. Hush: a cracked pedestal,
the hidden wiring of a palace room,
two guards caught trying to crack a safe,
ransack a rumpled mind ... . Too late to chafe—

a visit, a speech, and let a helicopter fly.
How could it happen that a golden boy
of public life, a man for whom the sky
was no limit at all, whom effort seemed to buoy,
now sits with aching mouth and throat and tongue
and rummages through half-disheveled files
of memory, while his opponent foils,
downs a stung king? Poets have long since sung
of kings who would judge a crime while the crime was theirs,
of anti-kings who botch the gifts of the realm,
of birth, of the spirit's innermost affairs,
and in the end find transcendental calm
in waving farewell, in hanging up the phone.
Music is piped in: *Afternoon of a Faun;*

viewer: walks by and silently observes
dark faces on the walls: portraits of Grover
Cleveland, of Woodrow Wilson, Herbert Hoover,
FDR, Johnson—worry, pomp, self-serve,
ambition in its forty-minus forms,
in frames as gold as infirm the frames of some.
Sustenance—power. A law firm, favorite-son
status: there it begins. Careers in film,
on farm, matter far more than form, the mean
proportional of gold in thought and act.
Yet who is to say? A soloist. He packed
so much into a life, he was a man.
China alone ... . Is he a mothballed colonel?
How do we tell? Insignia? Feelings funnel—

what do Paranoia and Paradise
share in common? Just flaming swords? Perhaps
but a moment's ill-considered lapse
of memory, a gap? A pair of dice
rolled for high stakes, a life turned subtly back,
with the illusion carefully maintained
that he lives forward still? Deferring pained
knowledge of years never lived out? Kings can lack
in hindsight. Viewer mulls meals of Presidents:
how one would toast his own muffins, another
insist on engraved silver, scones with butter,
an extra place setting, a plate with mints,
a samovar for tea, should a guest be late
(embossed, brown-silver trademark: *Watermate);*

other appointments, comforts. Viceroy Freud
to govern the citrus colonies of the passions,
a doctor, to reach in between water and ashes
and cure the feelings that we are. Why the feud
between *power* in one sense and the next?
Viewer looks out the window. What would kings
mean to him now? A child knew a crown, a kiss,
a bridge over a river; a sacred text,
his Shakespeare, *The Book of Kings, Quixote, Faust;*
then gods who rule our thoughts: the Buddha, the Christ,
spirits who come to live like us, to suffer;
a king whose head must overrule his heart,
the story of a despot who found deep hurt.
The secret is out, our penalty is stiffer:

the talks were taped before the king was born,
where water nixes wash and streams are forded
in advance, so that our earthly, sordid
picture show shows a grain's excess, of burn,
an overexposed portrait drenched with light,
vanished. Life: a videotape replayed.
So we bear fearful burns: an unemployed
monarch, a verbal fight into bitter night.
Out on the sliding California coast,
where it's hardly past one in the afternoon
when morning wakens sunburst-red Japan,
a lonely man is clowning with his past.
For him, no sun shall set after this last rising,
the Son of the Sun should be that enterprising.

Back to the set. The trembling screen goes white,
it sheds its clothes of black and gray and silver;
all that is left is commercials. Not a sliver
of decency around. But the bearish fight
is over for the night; the darker light,
regrets, faltering, tearful voices, are shut
away in their jack-o'-lantern boxes, but
for one week. Look, listen again as bright
entrepreneurs bring you a new installment
of pain, the most innocuous ingredient
in drama, not a play, a life too deep ... .
Viewer rubs his eyes at journalistic lore,
turns off the set, sinks to the ocean floor,
a powerless realm whose voices he hears in sleep.